Oh! My Phonics

2

Short Vowels

CEDU BOOK

INTRODUCTION

• WORD CHANT

The fun chants and captivating illustrations introduce the target sounds and words.

• LISTEN & REPEAT

Students can learn and practice the target sounds and words. They can also understand the letter-sound relationships.

• WORD READING

Students can practice reading words with the target sounds.

• WRITING

The target sounds and words can be strengthened through writing activities.

• LISTENING

Students can reinforce the target sounds and words through listening activities.

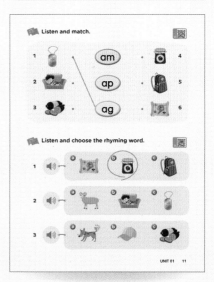

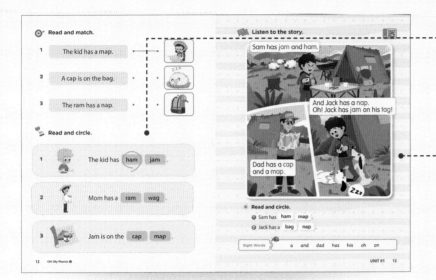

UNIT 01 13

• SENTENCE READING

Students can practice reading sentences with the target words.

• STORY READING

A phonics story offers students practice with reading target words in natural contexts. They can naturally improve their sight word reading skills.

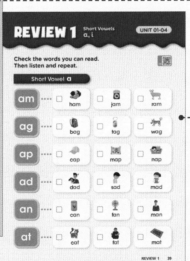

• UNIT QUIZ

Students can check what they have learned in the previous two units.

• REVIEW

A variety of activities can help students recall and further practice the sounds and words from previous units.

WORKBOOK

Students can reinforce what they have learned by completing the follow-up exercises featured in the accompanying workbook.

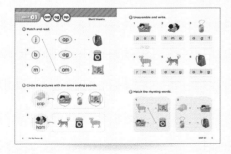

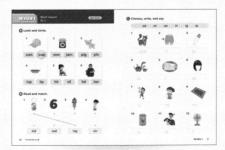

CONTENTS

6

am ag ap

Short Vowel a

Listen and chant.

ram

ham

jam

bag

cap

map

tag

wag

nap

Zzz

jam   **ham**   **ram**

bag   **tag**   **wag**

cap   **map**   **nap**

Say and circle.

1. ham
2. nap
3. wag
4. cap
5. jam
6. bag

Circle and write.

1 c （b a g） p m .... *bag*

2 d j a t a g ....

3 n a m n a p ....

4 m r a m p h ....

5 n h a m a p ....

6 w a g h a n ....

7 t j e c a p ....

Listen and match.

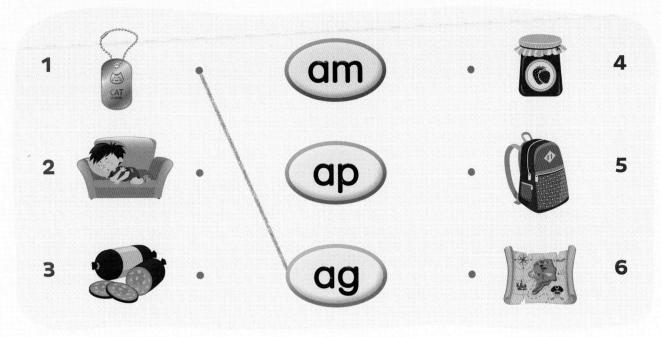

1   •   **am**   •   4

2   •   **ap**   •   5

3   •   **ag**   •   6

 Listen and choose the rhyming word.

1   a   b   c

2   a   b   c

3   a   b   c

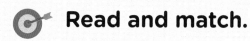 **Read and match.**

1 The kid has a **map.**

2 A **cap** is on the **bag.**

3 The **ram** has a **nap.**

 Read and circle.

1  The kid has (**ham**) **jam** .

2  Mom has a **ram** **wag** .

3 Jam is on the **cap** **map** .

Listen to the story.

Sam has jam and ham.

And Jack has a nap.
Oh! Jack has jam on his tag!

Dad has a cap and a map.

Zzz

☀ **Read and circle.**

1 Sam has   ham   map .

2 Jack has a   bag   nap .

Sight Words   a   and   dad   has   his   oh   on

QUIZ UNIT 01

A Listen and circle.

1

2

B Listen and check.

1 ☐ ram ☑ bag

2 ☐ tag ☐ jam

3 ☐ cap ☐ wag

4 ☐ nap ☐ ham

C Look, find, and circle.

1

2

3

4

w	d	c	a	p
m	a	a	r	n
a	m	g	a	a
p	a	n	m	t
h	j	a	m	j

dad   **sad**   **mad**

can   **fan**   **man**

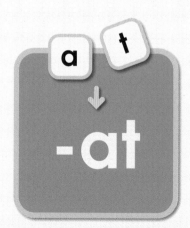

cat   **fat**   **mat**

Say and circle.

1 **can**

2 **fat**

3 **mad**

4 **fan**

5 **cat**

6 **sad**

Circle and write.

1   c   b   a   d   a   d   _____

2   f   a   t   n   a   c   _____

3   r   m   a   d   f   p   _____

4   h   a   t   m   a   t   _____

5   p   h   a   c   a   n   _____

6   s   a   c   a   t   a   _____

7   m   c   a   m   a   n   _____

Listen and match.

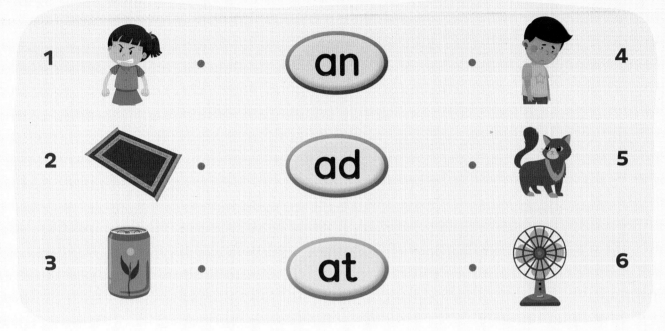

1   an   4

2   ad   5

3   at   6

 Listen and choose the rhyming word.

1   a   b   c

2   a   b   c

3   a   b   c

Read and match.

1 A **fan** is on the **mat.** • •

2 A **cat** is in the **can.** • •

3 The **man** is **mad.** • •

 Read and circle.

1 A [fat] [mad] cat.

2 The ram is on the [fan] [can] .

3 Dad is [mad] [sad] .

Listen to the story.

Dad is on the mat.
Dad looks sad.

A cat is on the mat.
A fat cat is on the mat.
The cat looks cute.

A man is on the mat.
The man looks mad.

☀ **Read and circle.**

❶ A fat can cat is on the mat.

❷ Dad looks mad sad .

Sight Words	a is looks on the

QUIZ UNIT 01-02

A Listen and circle.

1

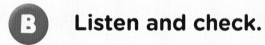

2

B Listen and check.

1 ☐ can ☐ mad   **2** ☐ bag ☐ jam

3 ☐ fat ☐ sad   **4** ☐ tag ☐ dad

C Look, find, and circle.

1   **2**

3   **4**

b	d	c	a	p
n	f	a	t	n
t	s	a	g	a
j	a	m	n	t
s	a	d	m	j

ig in ip

• Listen and chant.

pig

big

wig

fin

pin

win

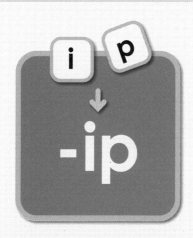

hip

lip

rip

Match and say.

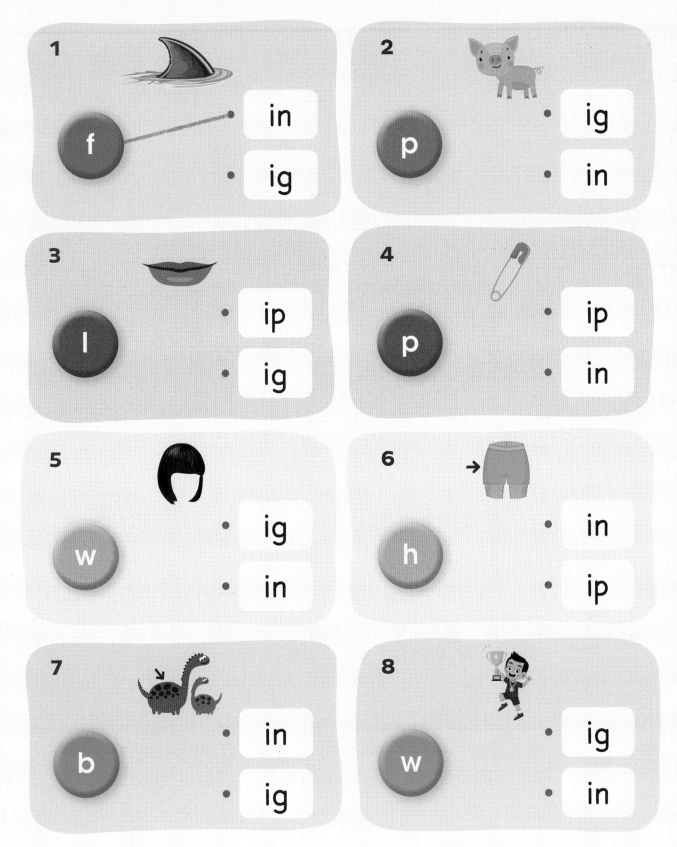

1
f
in
ig

2
p
ig
in

3
l
ip
ig

4
p
ip
in

5
w
ig
in

6
h
in
ip

7
b
in
ig

8
w
ig
in

Find, circle, and write.

1

_____

pig

2

_____

3

_____

4

_____

5

_____

6

→

_____

7

_____

s	r	e	x	b	i	g
l	i	n	m	t	t	b
a	i	a	b	h	i	p
m	h	p	m	x	k	i
l	r	i	p	d	a	n
w	i	g	e	f	i	n
p	q	w	i	n	w	m

8

_____

9

_____

Listen and color.

17

1
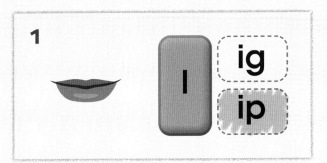

l | ig / ip

2

p | in / ig

3
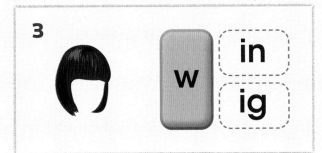

w | in / ig

4

f | ig / in

 Listen and number.

18

1 | 1 | | |

2 | | | |

3 | | | |

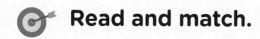 **Read and match.**

1 A **wig** is on the **pig**. •

2 A **pin** is on the **hip**. •

3 The kid has a **big** cat. •

 Read and circle.

1  The cats win   wig .

2  I lip   rip the map.

3 The pin   fin is red.

🎧 Listen to the story.

※ Read and circle.

1. There is a pig in a [**big**] [**wig**] .

2. The fish has [**fin**] [**pin**] s.

| Sight Words | a   am   hello   I   is   my   the   this   you |

QUIZ UNIT 02-03

ad, an, at, ig, in, ip

A Listen and circle.

1

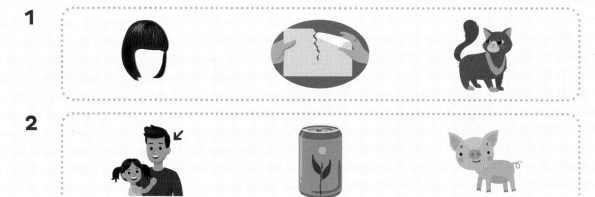

2

B Listen and check.

1 ☐ fin   ☐ fat   2 ☐ big   ☐ hip

3 ☐ win   ☐ fan   4 ☐ man   ☐ sad

C Look, find, and circle.

1   2

3   4

m	l	i	p	p
f	s	a	t	m
a	p	a	a	a
n	a	i	n	t
m	a	d	n	j

id it ix

Short Vowel i

• Listen and chant.

kid

lid

hit

sit

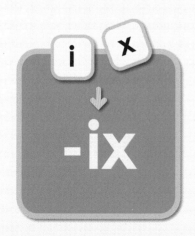

mix

fix

six

Match and say.

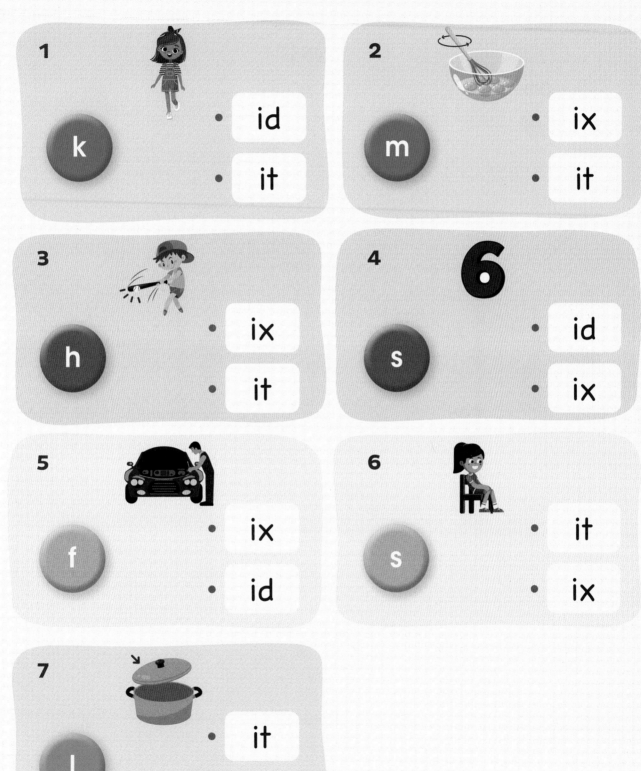

1 k
• id
• it

2 m
• ix
• it

3 h
• ix
• it

4 6 s
• id
• ix

5 f
• ix
• id

6 s
• it
• ix

7 l
• it
• id

Find, circle, and write.

1

6

_____

- - - - - - - - - - - -

_____

2

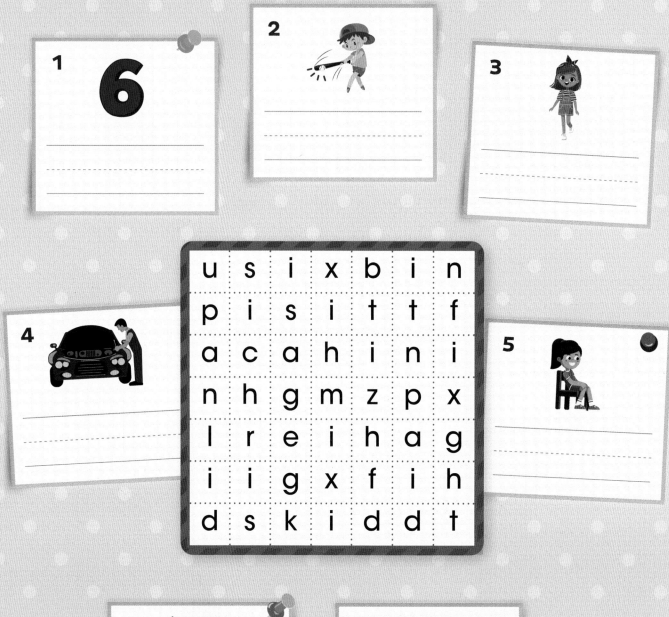

_____

- - - - - - - - - - - -

_____

3

_____

- - - - - - - - - - - -

_____

4

_____

- - - - - - - - - - - -

_____

u	s	i	x	b	i	n
p	i	s	i	t	t	f
a	c	a	h	i	n	i
n	h	g	m	z	p	x
l	r	e	i	h	a	g
i	i	g	x	f	i	h
d	s	k	i	d	d	t

5

_____

- - - - - - - - - - - -

_____

6

_____

- - - - - - - - - - - -

_____

7

_____

- - - - - - - - - - - -

_____

Listen and color.

1. h [ix] [it]

2. s [it] [id]

3. f [ix] [id]

4. k [it] [id]

 Listen and number.

1.

2.

3.

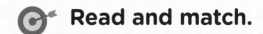 **Read and match.**

1 They **fix** the fan.   •   •

2 The **kid hits** the ball.   •   •

3 Six rams **sit** on the mat. •   •

 Read and circle.

1   A can on the   kid   lid .

2   I   fix   mix   the eggs.

3   The kids   sit   hit   on the bed.

Listen to the story.

The kids sit on the mat.
The kids fix the robot.
They have fun!

The kids hit the cans.
They have fun!

The kids mix the eggs.
They have fun!

☀ **Read and circle.**

① The kids [mix] [fix] the robot.

② The kids [hit] [sit] the cans.

Sight Words   have   on   the   they

QUIZ UNIT 03-04

A Listen and circle.

1

2

B Listen and check.

1
☐ hit ☐ pig

2
☐ six ☐ kid

3
☐ rip ☐ win

4
☐ pin ☐ sit

C Look, find, and circle.

1  2

3 4

f	d	l	x	p
i	f	h	i	t
x	w	i	g	d
l	i	t	i	n
h	i	p	p	j

29

Check the words you can read.
Then listen and repeat.

Short Vowel a

am	☐ ham	☐ jam	☐ ram
ag	☐ bag	☐ tag	☐ wag
ap	☐ cap	☐ map	☐ nap
ad	☐ dad	☐ sad	☐ mad
an	☐ can	☐ fan	☐ man
at	☐ cat	☐ fat	☐ mat

Check the words you can read.
Then listen and repeat.

Short Vowel i

ig ·····
- [ ] pig
- [ ] big
- [ ] wig

in ·····
- [ ] fin
- [ ] pin
- [ ] win

ip ·····
- [ ] hip
- [ ] lip
- [ ] rip

id ·····
- [ ] kid
- [ ] lid

it ·····
- [ ] hit
- [ ] sit

ix ·····
- [ ] mix
- [ ] fix
- [ ] **6** six

A

Listen and circle.

1

2 →

3

B

Listen, circle, and check.

1

☐	☐	☑
cap	cat	can

2

☐	☐	☐
wig	win	wag

C Say and color.

Short Vowel a

Short Vowel i

D Listen and check.

1

2

3

4

E Listen and circle.

1 A  is on the mat.

2 A   is on the lid.

3 The pig has a   .

4 The   is sad.

F Find the rhyming words and write the numbers.

G What does not rhyme? Find and cross out.

H   Look and write.

1

A ___ram___ has a ___nap___ .

2

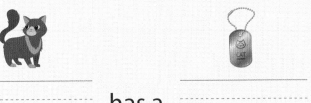

The _____ has a _____ .

3

A _____ is on the _____ .

4

The _____ is on the _____ .

5

6

_____ pins are on the _____ .

1 Write the words in the correct column.

Words with Short Vowel **a**	Words with Short Vowel **i**
fan	pig

- Listen and chant.

Ted

1, 2, ...10!

ten

Ted's Farm

hen

vet

pet

wet

red

bed

pen

-ed

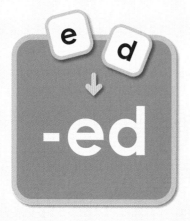

bed

red

Ted

-en

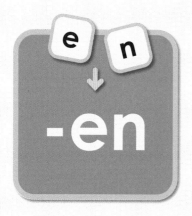

hen

ten

pen

-et

pet

vet

wet

Say and circle.

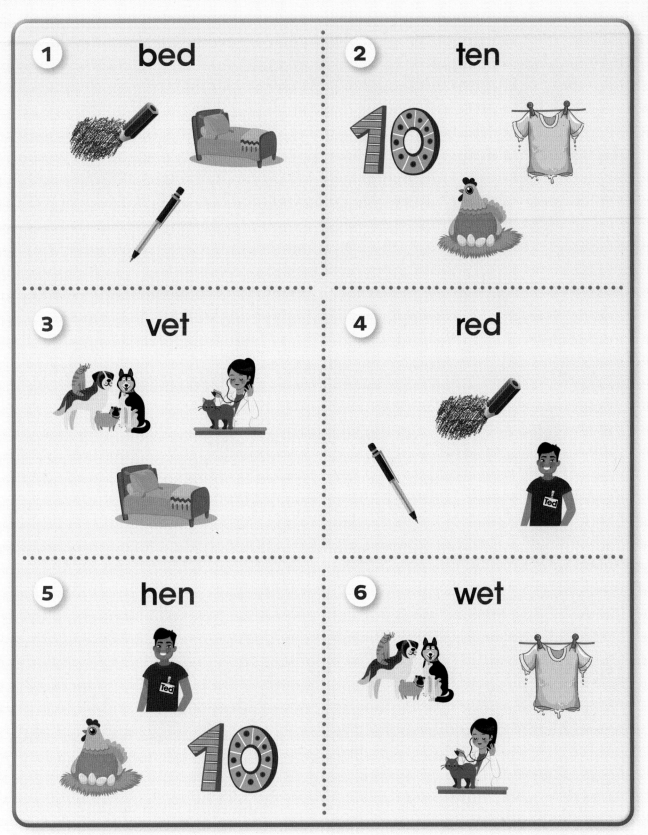

1 bed	**2** ten
3 vet	**4** red
5 hen	**6** wet

Circle and write.

1 a c t e n d _____

2 v a t v e t _____

3 r e d n e p _____

4 h e n h e t _____

5 w p e n e t _____

6 n b i w e t _____

7 b e p e t n _____

Listen and match.

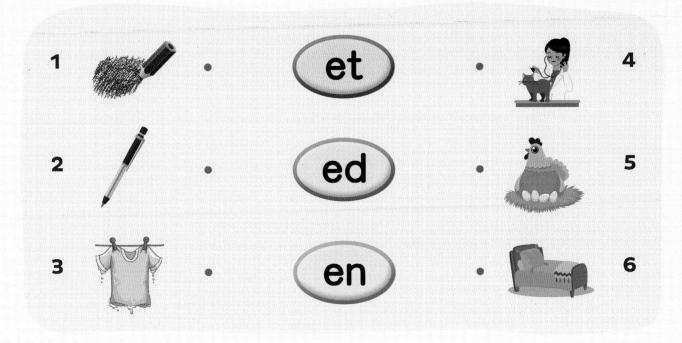

1   •   **et**   •   4

2   •   **ed**   •   5

3   •   **en**   •   6

 Listen and choose the rhyming word.

1   a   b   c

2   a   b   c

3   a   b   c

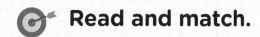 **Read and match.**

1 The **vet** is **wet.** • •

2 **Ted** has a **red** bag. • •

3 **Ten hen**s are on the **bed.** • •

 Read and circle.

1 A dog is on the | bed | pen | .

2 The cap is | red | hen | .

3 I have | pet | ten | cans.

※ **Read and circle.**

1. Ted has [ten] [pen] hens.

2. Peg is a [wet] [vet] .

Sight Words   a   has   is   look   too

QUIZ UNIT 04-05

A Listen and circle.

1

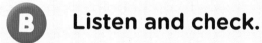

2

B Listen and check.

1 ☐ vet ☐ pen
2 ☐ kid ☐ red
3 ☐ fix ☐ mix
4 ☐ hen ☐ hit

C Look, find, and circle.

1
2
3
4

s	d	c	a	t
i	r	a	e	r
x	e	w	a	m
h	t	e	n	l
s	j	s	i	t

Listen and chant.

fox

log

dog

Aaahh...

ox

fog

box

dot

hot

pot

dog

log

fog

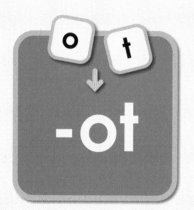

hot

pot

dot

box

fox

ox

Say and circle.

1 dog

2 fox

3 dot

4 ox

5 log

6 hot

Circle and write.

1 g f o x n t _____

2  t q t p o t _____

3 r f o g e i _____

4 b e x b o x _____

5 s j e o x a _____

6 w a w l o g _____

7 h o t n o t _____

Listen and match.

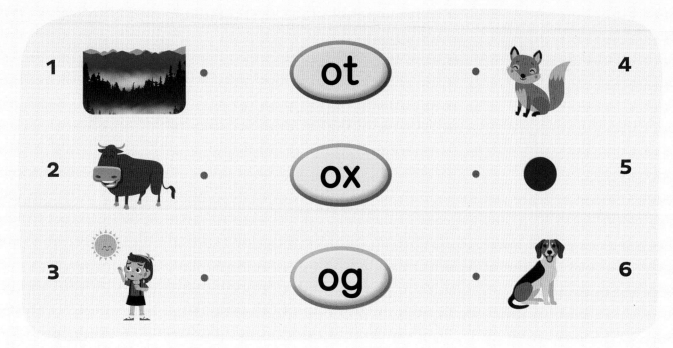

1

2

3

ot

ox

og

4

5

6

 Listen and choose the rhyming word.

1   a   b   c

2   a   b   c

3   a   b   c

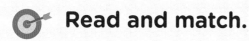 **Read and match.**

1 The **box** has **dots**.

2 The man has a **log**.

3 The **pot** is **hot**.

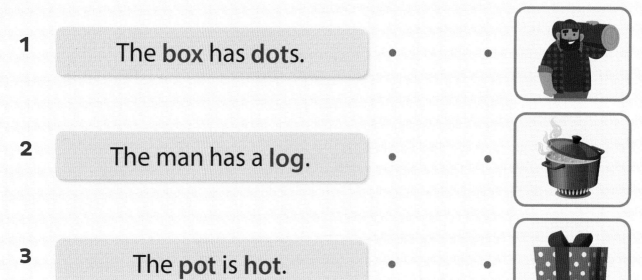

 Read and circle.

1 A dog is on the **log** **fog** .

2 A pot is in the **fox** **box** .

3 A boy has a **pot** **hot** .

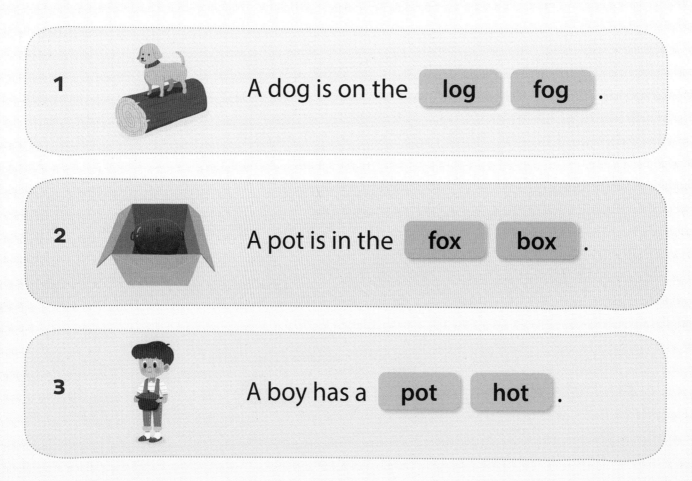

A dog is on the log.
A fox is on the log.

Aaahh...

Now the dog is on the box.
Where is the fox?

And an ox is on the log!

Oh no!
The fox is on the hot pot!

☀ **Read and circle.**

❶ A fox is on the   dog   log .

❷ The dog is on the   box   pot .

Sight Words	a an and is no now oh on the where

QUIZ UNIT 05-06

A Listen and circle.

1

2

B Listen and check.

1 ☐ dot ☐ pot   **2** ☐ vet ☐ wet

3 ☐ hen ☐ ten   **4** ☐ box ☐ bed

C Look, find, and circle.

1 **2**

3 **4**

f	d	h	d	i
g	r	a	o	r
t	e	n	g	t
d	d	r	h	e
s	p	e	n	t

ug un up

49

- Listen and chant.

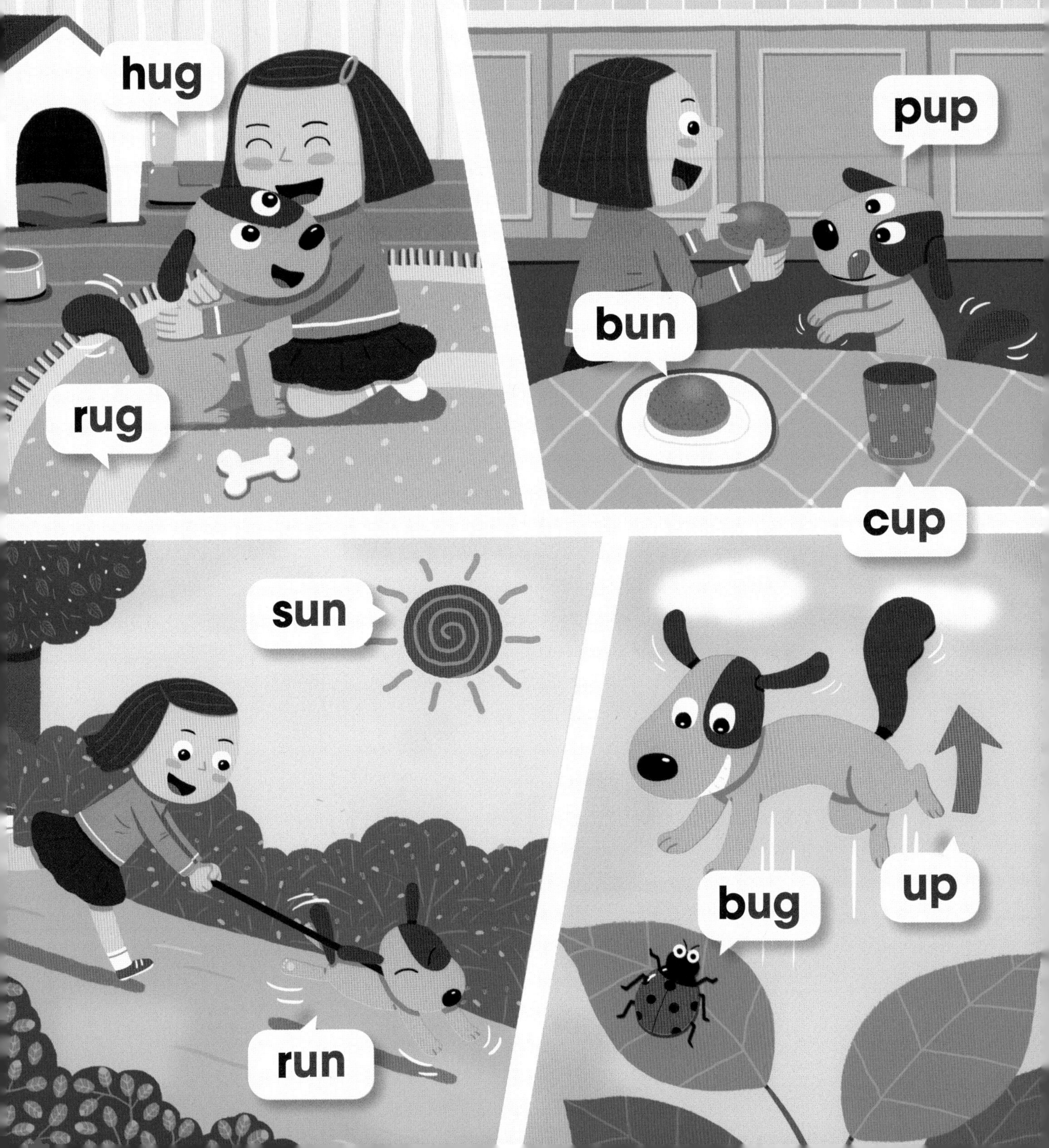

bug　　　**hug**　　　**rug**

sun　　　**bun**　　　**run**

up　　　**cup**　　　**pup**

Match and say.

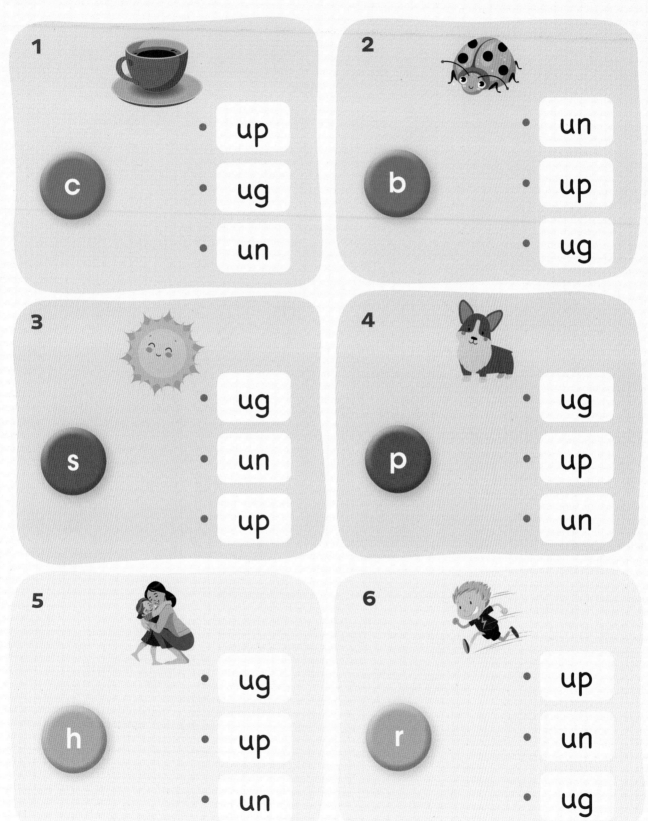

1 · up
  c · ug
    · un

2 · un
  b · up
    · ug

3 · ug
  s · un
    · up

4 · ug
  p · up
    · un

5 · ug
  h · up
    · un

6 · up
  r · un
    · ug

Find, circle, and write.

1

2

3

4

s	q	i	u	m	u	p
r	u	g	m	t	e	g
s	a	n	l	p	u	p
u	h	b	u	n	p	i
j	r	u	a	d	a	g
z	g	n	g	r	u	n
b	u	g	i	c	u	p

5

6

7

8

9

Listen and color.

1

c — ug / up

2

h — up / ug

3

r — ug / un

4
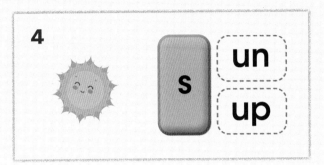
s — un / up

 Listen and number.

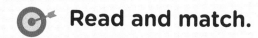 **Read and match.**

1   A **bug** is on the **rug**.   •   •

2   The kids jump **up**.   •   •

3   A **pup run**s to the **bun**.   •   •

 Read and circle.

1   The two pups   rug   hug .

2   A bug is on the   cup   pup .

3   I see the   sun   bun .

Listen to the story.

☀ **Read and circle.**

① The kid hugs the [bun] [pup] .

② The pup likes to [run] [sun] .

Sight Words: he I is jump likes my this to

QUIZ UNIT 06-07

A Listen and circle.

1

2

B Listen and check.

1 ☐ bun ☐ fox   **2** ☐ pup ☐ bug

3 ☐ dog ☐ rug   **4** ☐ up ☐ hot

C Look, find, and circle.

1 **2**

3 **4**

k	d	h	u	g
n	f	a	o	n
b	n	f	a	r
f	o	h	o	u
r	a	x	p	n

-ub

tub　　**rub**

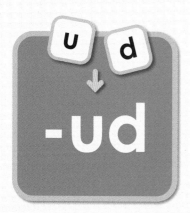

-ud

bud　　**mud**

-ut

cut　　**nut**　　**hut**

Match and say.

1

ud

ut

ub

2

ut

ub

ud

3

ud

ub

ut

4

ut

ud

ub

5

ut

ub

ud

6

ud

ut

ub

Find, circle, and write.

1

2

3

4

5

6

7

Listen and color.

1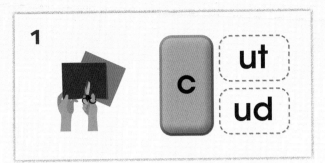

c

ut

ud

2

m

ud

ut

3

r

ud

ub

4

t

ub

ud

Listen and number.

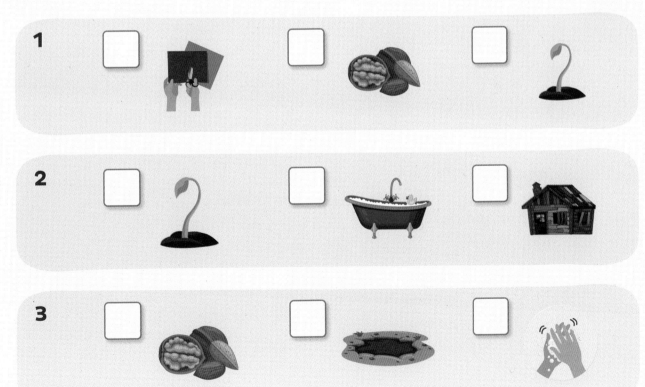

 **Read and match.**

1 The **nut**s are in the cup. • •

2 We play in the **mud**. • •

3 I **cut** the bun. • •

 Read and circle.

1 Two pigs are in the   mud   cut .

2 We run to the   nut   hut .

3 The pup is in the   mud   tub .

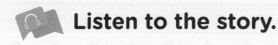 **Listen to the story.**

☀ **Read and circle.**

1 They find a   **bud**   **hut**   .

2 They   **cut**   **rub**   the tub.

Sight Words	a are big find oh the they where

QUIZ UNIT 07-08

A Listen and circle.

1
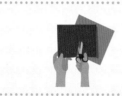

2

B Listen and check.

1 ☐ cup ☐ cut

2 ☐ sun ☐ hug

3 ☐ up ☐ hut

4 ☐ rub ☐ tub

C Look, find, and circle.

1

2

3

4

c	n	m	u	d
a	u	a	o	n
b	t	b	u	g
n	o	h	o	t
r	b	u	n	j

REVIEW 2

Short Vowels
e, o, u

Check the words you can read.
Then listen and repeat.

Short Vowel e

ed	☐ bed	☐ red	☐ Ted
en	☐ hen	☐ ten	☐ pen
et	☐ pet	☐ vet	☐ wet

Short Vowel o

og	☐ dog	☐ log	☐ fog
ot	☐ hot	☐ pot	☐ dot
ox	☐ box	☐ fox	☐ ox

Check the words you can read.
Then listen and repeat.

Short Vowel u

ug ····
- ☐ 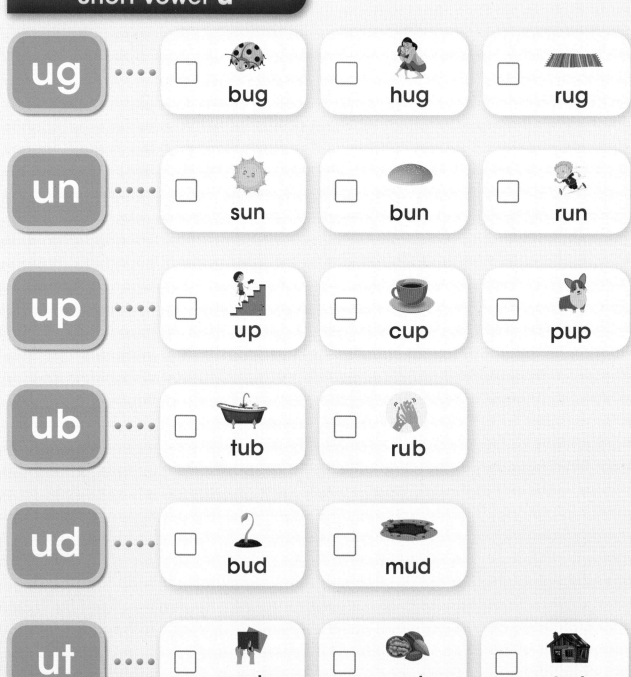 bug
- ☐ hug
- ☐ rug

un ····
- ☐ sun
- ☐ bun
- ☐ run

up ····
- ☐ up
- ☐ cup
- ☐ pup

ub ····
- ☐ tub
- ☐ rub

ud ····
- ☐ bud
- ☐ mud

ut ····
- ☐ cut
- ☐ nut
- ☐ hut

A Listen and circle.

65

1

2

3

B Listen, circle, and check.

66

1

☐	☐	☑
bud	bug	bed

2

☐	☐	☐
hut	hen	hot

3

☐	☐	☐
red	rug	run

C **Say and color.**

Short Vowel e   Short Vowel o

pen

box

dot

red

pet

dog

wet

log

Short Vowel u

 fog

 sun

 ox

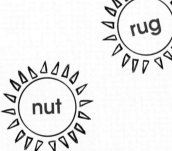 nut

rug

 cup

 tub

 ten

 bun

D Listen and check.

1  2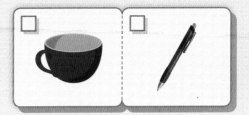

3 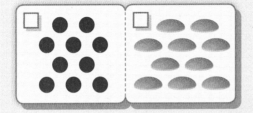 4

E Listen and circle.

1 A  is in the box.

2 The kids   the mat.

3 The   is hot.

4 The pup is on the   .

REVIEW 2   83

F Find the rhyming words and write the numbers.

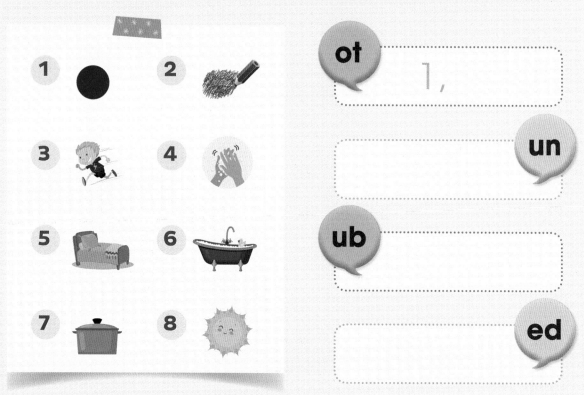

G What does not rhyme? Find and cross out.

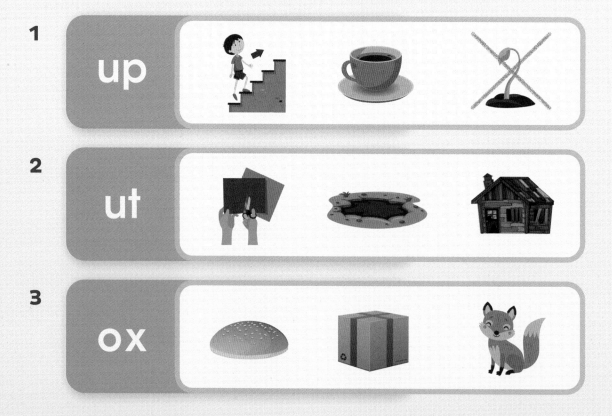

H **Look and write.**

1

The ___bug___ is in the ___cup___ .

2

The _____ is _____ .

3

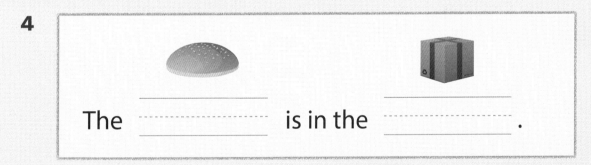

The _____ runs to the _____ .

4

The _____ is in the _____ .

5

The _____ is _____ .

1 **Write the words in the correct column.**

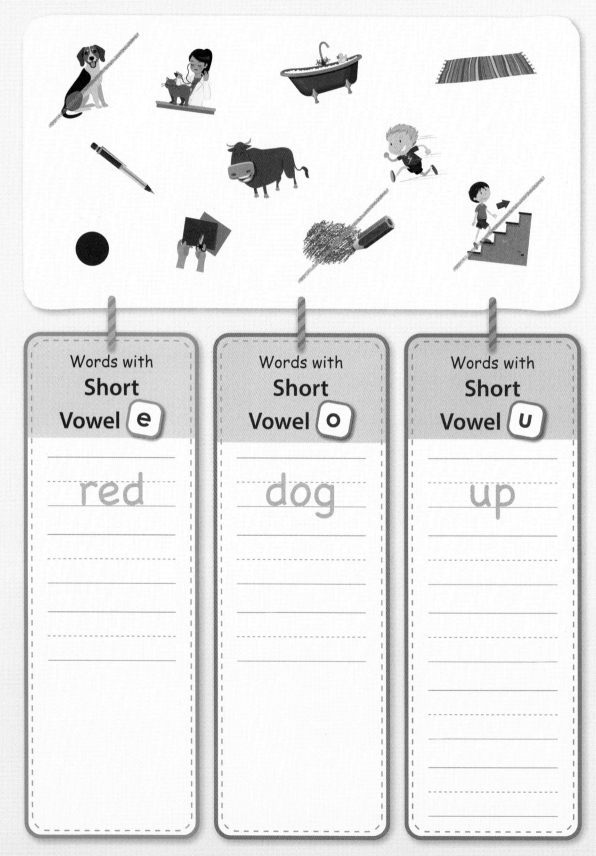

Words with **Short Vowel** e	Words with **Short Vowel** o	Words with **Short Vowel** u
red	dog	up

WORD LIST

• **Can you read? Read and check.**

UNIT 01

1. ☐ jam
2. ☐ ham
3. ☐ ram
4. ☐ bag
5. ☐ tag
6. ☐ wag
7. ☐ cap
8. ☐ map
9. ☐ nap

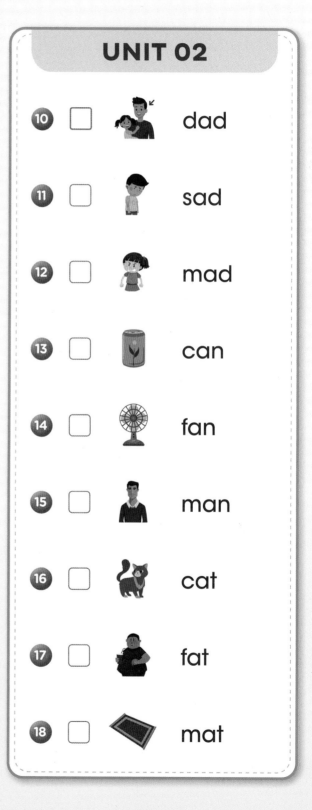

UNIT 02

10. ☐ dad
11. ☐ sad
12. ☐ mad
13. ☐ can
14. ☐ fan
15. ☐ man
16. ☐ cat
17. ☐ fat
18. ☐ mat

UNIT 03

19 ☐ pig

20 ☐ big

21 ☐ wig

22 ☐ fin

23 ☐ pin

24 ☐ win

25 ☐ hip

26 ☐ lip

27 ☐ rip

UNIT 04

28 ☐ kid

29 ☐ lid

30 ☐ hit

31 ☐ sit

32 ☐ mix

33 ☐ fix

34 ☐ **6** six

WORD LIST

• **Can you read? Read and check.**

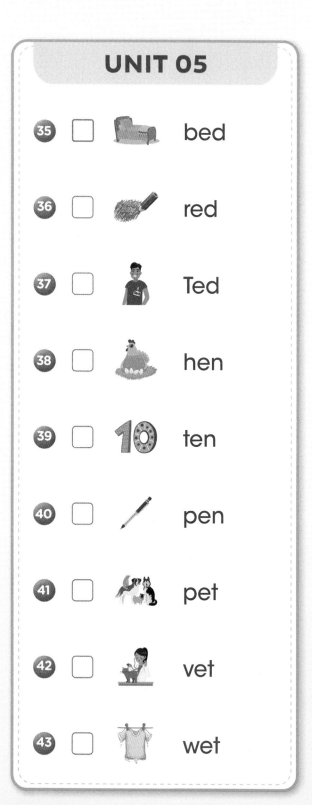

35	☐	bed
36	☐	red
37	☐	Ted
38	☐	hen
39	☐	ten
40	☐	pen
41	☐	pet
42	☐	vet
43	☐	wet

UNIT 05

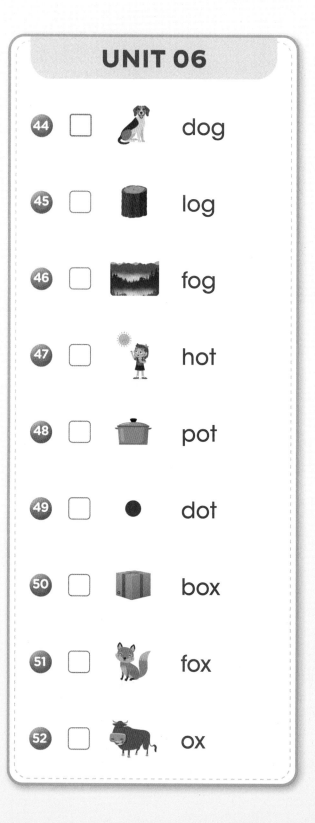

44	☐	dog
45	☐	log
46	☐	fog
47	☐	hot
48	☐	pot
49	☐	dot
50	☐	box
51	☐	fox
52	☐	ox

UNIT 06

UNIT 07

53 ☐ bug

54 ☐ hug

55 ☐ rug

56 ☐ sun

57 ☐ bun

58 ☐ run

59 ☐ up

60 ☐ cup

61 ☐ pup

UNIT 08

62 ☐ tub

63 ☐ rub

64 ☐ bud

65 ☐ mud

66 ☐ cut

67 ☐ nut

68 ☐ hut

SIGHT WORD LIST

• **Can you read? Read and check.**

1 ☐ a   13, 21, 29, 53, 61, 77

2 ☐ am   29

3 ☐ an   61

4 ☐ and   13, 61

5 ☐ are   77

6 ☐ big   77

7 ☐ dad   13

8 ☐ find   77

9 ☐ has   13, 53

10 ☐ have   37

11 ☐ he   69

12 ☐ hello   29

13 ☐ his   13

14 ☐ I   29, 69

15 ☐ is   21, 29, 53, 61, 69

16 ☐ jump   69

17 ☐ likes   69

18 ☐ look   53

19 ☐ looks   21

20 ☐ my   29, 69

21 ☐ no   61

22 ☐ now   61

23 ☐ oh   13, 61, 77

24 ☐ on   13, 21, 37, 61

25 ☐ the   21, 29, 37, 61, 77

26 ☐ they   37, 77

27 ☐ this   29, 69

28 ☐ to   69

29 ☐ too   53

30 ☐ where   61, 77

31 ☐ you   29

SCOPE & SEQUENCE

Book 1 — Alphabet Sounds

UNIT 01	Aa Bb Cc
UNIT 02	Dd Ee Ff
UNIT 03	Gg Hh Ii
UNIT 04	Jj Kk Ll
UNIT 05	Mm Nn Oo
UNIT 06	Pp Qq Rr
UNIT 07	Ss Tt Uu Vv
UNIT 08	Ww Xx Yy Zz

Book 2 — Short Vowels

UNIT 01	Short Vowel a: am, ag, ap
UNIT 02	Short Vowel a: ad, an, at
UNIT 03	Short Vowel i: ig, in, ip
UNIT 04	Short Vowel i: id, it, ix
UNIT 05	Short Vowel e: ed, en, et
UNIT 06	Short Vowel o: og, ot, ox
UNIT 07	Short Vowel u: ug, un, up
UNIT 08	Short Vowel u: ub, ud, ut

Book 3 — Long Vowels

UNIT 01	Short Vowels Review
UNIT 02	Long Vowel a: a_e
UNIT 03	Long Vowel a: a_e
UNIT 04	Long Vowel i: i_e
UNIT 05	Long Vowel i: i_e
UNIT 06	Long Vowel o: o_e
UNIT 07	Long Vowel o: o_e
UNIT 08	Long Vowel u: u_e

Book 4 — Double Letters

UNIT 01	Consonant Blends : bl, fl, gl, sl
UNIT 02	Consonant Blends : br, cr, dr, gr
UNIT 03	Consonant Blends : sm, sn, st, sw
UNIT 04	Consonant Digraphs : sh, ch, th, ng
UNIT 05	Vowel Digraphs : ai, ay Vowel Diphthongs : oi, oy
UNIT 06	Vowel Digraphs : oa, ow1 (snow) Vowel Diphthongs : ou, ow2 (cow)
UNIT 07	R-controlled Vowels : ar, or, ir, er
UNIT 08	Vowel Digraphs: ee, ea, short oo, long oo

MEMO

MEMO

Flashcards

with SAYPEN

UNIT 01

UNIT 01
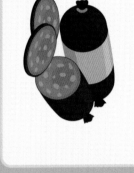

UNIT 01

UNIT 02

UNIT 01

UNIT 01

UNIT 02

UNIT 02

UNIT 01
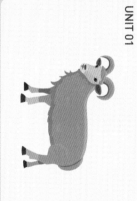

UNIT 01

UNIT 02

UNIT 02

UNIT 01

UNIT 01
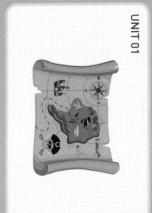

UNIT 02

UNIT 02

jam	ham	ram	bag
SAYPEN	SAYPEN	SAYPEN	SAYPEN
tag	wag	cap	map
SAYPEN	SAYPEN	SAYPEN	SAYPEN
nap	dad	sad	mad
SAYPEN	SAYPEN	SAYPEN	SAYPEN
can	fan	man	cat
SAYPEN	SAYPEN	SAYPEN	SAYPEN

UNIT 04

UNIT 05

UNIT 05

UNIT 06

UNIT 04

UNIT 05

UNIT 05

UNIT 06

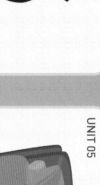

UNIT 05

UNIT 05

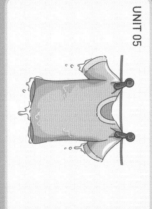

UNIT 05

UNIT 06

UNIT 05

UNIT 06

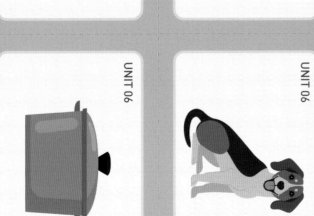

UNIT 06

UNIT 06

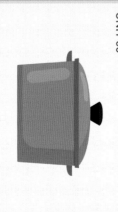

UNIT 06

red	bed	six	fix
pen	ten	hen	Ted
dog	wet	vet	pet
pot	hot	fog	log

UNIT 07

UNIT 07

UNIT 07

UNIT 06

UNIT 08

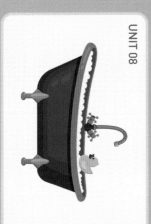

UNIT 07

UNIT 07

UNIT 06

UNIT 08

UNIT 07

UNIT 07

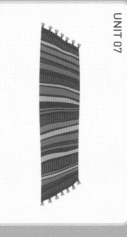

UNIT 06

UNIT 08

UNIT 07

UNIT 07

UNIT 06

dot

bug

bun

pup

box

hug

run

tub

fox

rug

up

rub

ox

sun

cup

bud

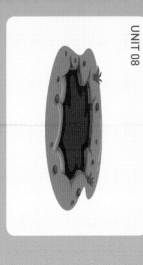

UNIT 08

UNIT 08

UNIT 08

UNIT 08

mud

cut

nut

hut

with 세이펜

원어민 발음을
실시간 반복학습

단어 및 문장의
우리말 해석 듣기

발음을 듣고 따라 해보며
혼자서도 쉽게 학습

세이펜 핀파일 다운로드 안내

STEP ① 세이펜과 컴퓨터를 USB 케이블로 연결하세요.

STEP ② 쎄듀북 홈페이지(www.cedubook.com)에 접속 후, 학습자료실 메뉴에서 학습할 교재를 찾아 이동합니다.

> 초등교재 ▶ ELT ▶ 학습교재 클릭 ▶ 세이펜 핀파일 자료 클릭
> ▶ 다운로드 (저장을 '다른 이름으로 저장'으로 변경하여 저장소를 USB로 변경) ▶ 완료

STEP ③ 음원 다운로드가 완료되면 세이펜과 컴퓨터의 USB 케이블을 분리하세요.

STEP ④ 세이펜을 분리하면 "시스템을 초기화 중입니다. 잠시만 기다려 주세요."라는 멘트가 나옵니다.

STEP ⑤ 멘트 종료 후 세이펜을 〈Oh! My Phonics〉 표지에 대보세요.
효과음이 나온 후 바로 학습을 시작할 수 있습니다.

참고사항

◆ 세이펜은 본 교재에 포함되어 있지 않습니다. 별도로 구매하여 이용할 수 있으며, 기존에 보유하신 세이펜이 있다면 핀파일만 다운로드해서
바로 이용하실 수 있습니다.

◆ 세이펜에서 제작된 모든 기종(기존에 보유하고 계신 기종도 호환 가능)으로 사용이 가능합니다.

◆ 모든 기종은 세이펜에서 권장하는 최신 펌웨어 업데이트를 진행해 주시기 바랍니다.
업데이트는 세이펜 홈페이지(www.saypen.com)에서 가능합니다.

◆ 핀파일은 쎄듀북 홈페이지(www.cedubook.com)와 세이펜 홈페이지(www.saypen.com)에서 모두 다운로드 가능합니다.

◆ 세이펜을 이용하지 않는 학습자는 쎄듀북 홈페이지 부가학습자료, 교재 내 QR코드 이미지 등을 활용하여 원어민 음성으로 학습하실 수 있습니다.

◆ 기타 문의사항은 www.cedubook.com / 02-3272-4766으로 연락 바랍니다.

세이펜과 함께 배우는 Oh! My Phonics

〈Oh! My Phonics〉의 Student Book과 부록 플래시카드에는 세이펜이 적용되어 있습니다. 세이펜을 가져다 대기만 하면 원어민의 생생한 영어 발음과 억양을 듣고 영어 말하기 연습을 할 수 있습니다.

*번역 기능 | 세이펜으로 책을 찍어서 원어민 음성을 들은 후, T 버튼을 짧게 누르면 우리말 해석 음원을 들을 수 있습니다.

🖊 세이펜을 대면 Activity의 지시문을 들을 수 있습니다. T 기능 지원

🖊 유닛에서 배우게 될 글자에 세이펜을 대면 원어민의 정확한 발음을 들을 수 있습니다.

🖊 QR코드에 세이펜을 대면 해당 트랙의 MP3 파일이 재생됩니다.

🖊 각 단어나 그림에 세이펜을 대면 원어민의 정확한 발음과 억양을 들을 수 있습니다. T 기능 지원

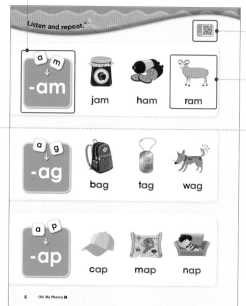

🖊 각 단어나 그림에 세이펜을 대면 원어민의 정확한 발음과 억양을 들을 수 있습니다. T 기능 지원

🖊 Listening 활동의 문제 번호에 펜을 대면 해당 문항의 음원이 재생됩니다.

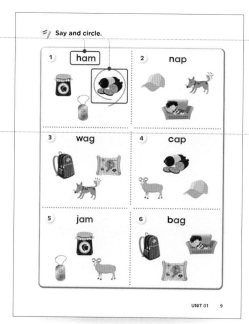

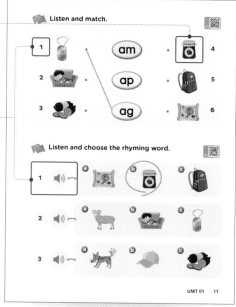

Oh! My Phonics

2

Short Vowels

Workbook

CEDU BOOK

Oh! My Phonics

2

Short Vowels

Workbook

CEDU BOOK

CONTENTS

A Match and read.

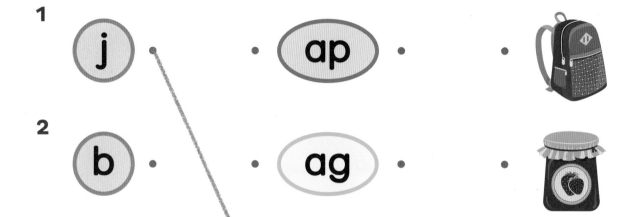

1   j   •   •   ap   •   •   [backpack]

2   b   •   •   ag   •   •   [jam]

3   m   •   •   am   •   •   [map]

B Circle the pictures with the same ending sounds.

1   cap   —○   [boy on sofa]   [cat tag]   [map]

2   ham   —○   [dog]   [jam]   [ram]

C Unscramble and write.

1

p a n

—— nap ——

2

h m a

3

a g t

4

r m a

5

a w g

6

a b g

D Match the rhyming words.

1

2

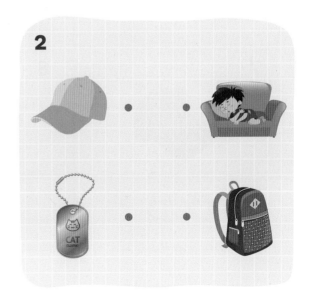

E Trace and write.

1
bag

2
tag

3
wag

4
ham

5
jam

6
ram

7
cap

8
nap

9
map

F Choose and write.

-am	-ag	-ap
ham		

G Read the sentences three times.

1 A **cap** is on the **bag**. ☐ ☐ ☐

2 The **ram** has a **nap**. ☐ ☐ ☐

3 **Jam** is on the **map**. ☐ ☐ ☐

A Match and read.

1   m ·   · at ·   ·

2   s ·   · ad ·   ·

3   f ·   · an ·   ·

B Circle the pictures with the same ending sounds.

1   cat

2   can

C Unscramble and write.

1

d d a
_____

2
d s a
_____

3
a c t
_____

4
f n a
_____

5
a m t
_____

6
a c n
_____

D Match the rhyming words.

1

2

E Trace and write.

1
can

2
fan

3
man

4
cat

5
fat

6
mat

7
dad

8
sad

9
mad

F Choose and write.

-an	-ad	-at

G Read the sentences three times.

1 The **man** is **mad**. ☐ ☐ ☐

2 A **fat cat** is on the **mat**. ☐ ☐ ☐

3 A **cat** is in the **can**. ☐ ☐ ☐

A Match and read.

1

 p ·   · ip ·   ·

2

 r ·   · in ·   ·

3

 f ·   · ig ·   ·

B Circle the pictures with the same ending sounds.

1

 wig

2

 fin

C Unscramble and write.

1

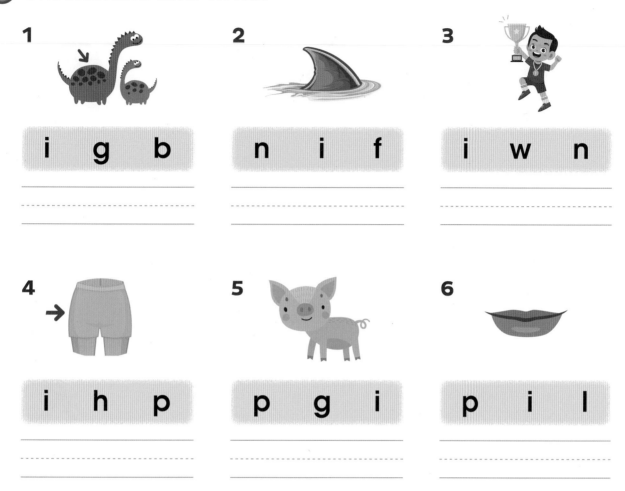

| i | g | b |

_____

2

| n | i | f |

_____

3

| i | w | n |

_____

4

| i | h | p |

_____

5

| p | g | i |

_____

6

| p | i | l |

_____

D Match the rhyming words.

1

2

E Trace and write.

1
pig

2
big

3
wig

4
fin

5
pin

6
win

7
hip

8
lip

9
rip

F Choose and write.

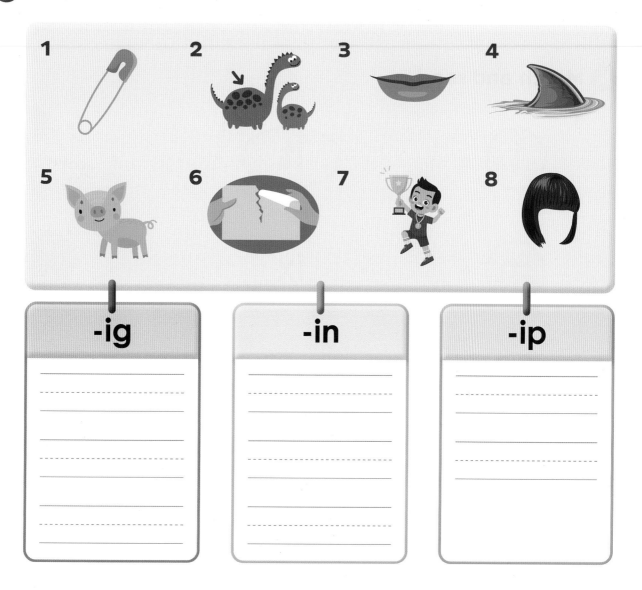

-ig	-in	-ip

G Read the sentences three times.

1 A **pin** is on the **hip**. ☐ ☐ ☐

2 A **wig** is on the **pig**. ☐ ☐ ☐

3 The **big fin** is red. ☐ ☐ ☐

A Match and read.

1

l · · it ·

2

m · · ix ·

3

h · · id ·

B Circle and say.

1 **id**

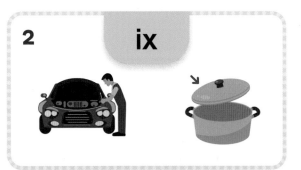

2 **ix**

3 **it**

4 **ix**

C Unscramble and write.

1

6

i s x

_____

2

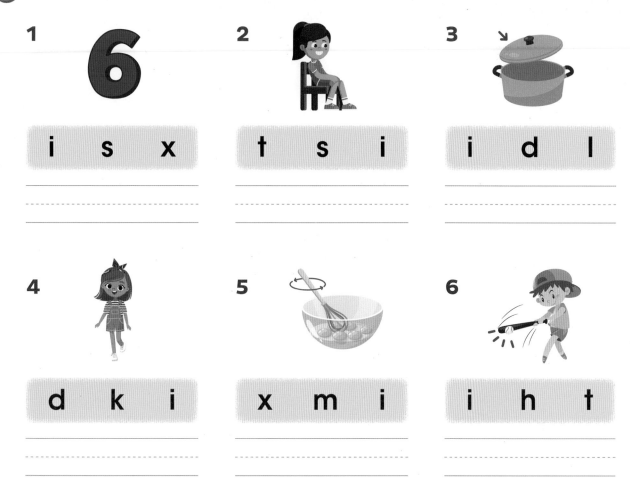

t s i

_____

3

i d l

_____

4

d k i

_____

5

x m i

_____

6

i h t

_____

D Match the rhyming words.

1

2

E Trace and write.

1

kid

2

lid

3

hit

4

sit

5

mix

6

fix

7

6

six

F Choose and write.

-id	-it	-ix

G Read the sentences three times.

1 They **fix** the fan. ☐ ☐ ☐

2 The **kid hit**s the ball. ☐ ☐ ☐

3 **Six** rams **sit** on the mat. ☐ ☐ ☐

A Look and circle.

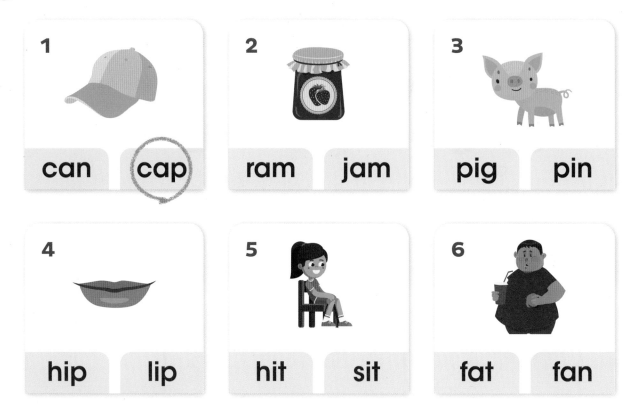

1 can (cap)

2 ram jam

3 pig pin

4 hip lip

5 hit sit

6 fat fan

B Read and match.

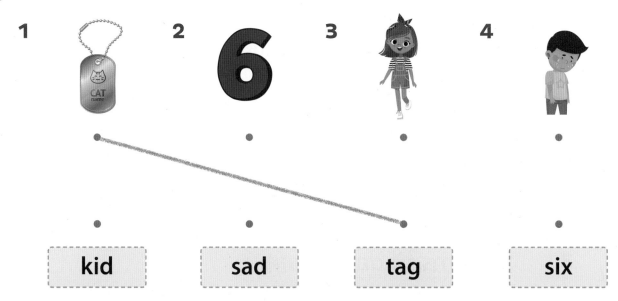

1   2   3   4

kid   sad   tag   six

C Choose, write, and say.

| ad | at | an | in | ig | ip |

1

cat

2

h

3

p

4

b

5

r

6

w

7

w

8

m

9

m

10

c

11

d

12

f

D Find and circle.

1

c	b	s	a	p
h	a	m	a	n

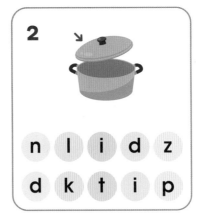

2

n	l	i	d	z
d	k	t	i	p

3

f	m	a	p	g
i	p	h	e	l

4

w	i	m	i	x
j	k	s	i	t

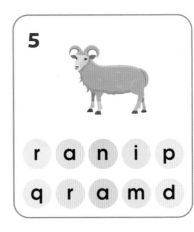

5

r	a	n	i	p
q	r	a	m	d

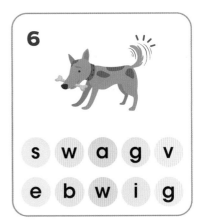

6

s	w	a	g	v
e	b	w	i	g

E Circle the pictures with the matching sound.

1

2

F Read, circle, and write.

1 Six pigs have a nap.

Sad   (Six)   Sit

2 A tag is on the _____ .

big   bag   cap

3 A cat is on the _____ .

mad   mix   mat

4 The _____ has a big cat.

wig   kid   pin

5 A _____ is on the lid.

cap   can   cat

A Match and read.

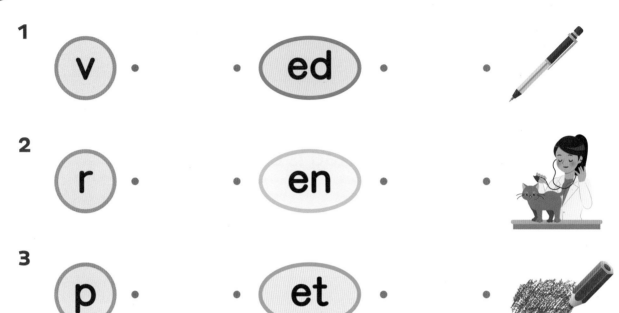

1 v •   • ed •   •

2 r •   • en •   •

3 p •   • et •   •

B Circle the pictures with the same ending sounds.

1 hen

2 pet

C Unscramble and write.

1

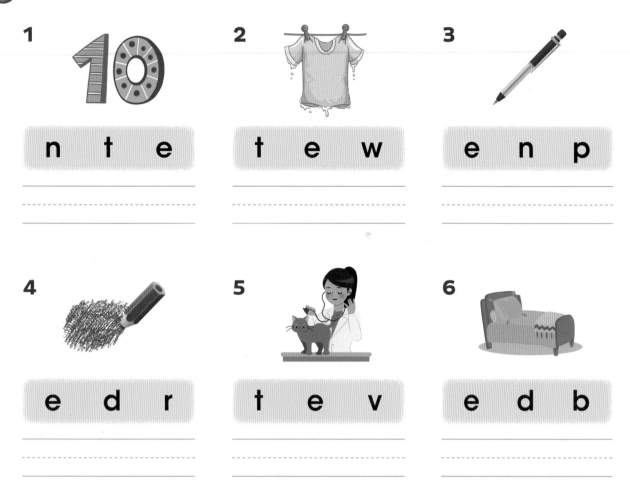

n	t	e

2

t	e	w

3

e	n	p

4

e	d	r

5

t	e	v

6

e	d	b

D Match the rhyming words.

1

2

Trace and write.

1

pet

2

vet

3

wet

4

bed

5

red

6

Ted

7

hen

8

ten

9

pen

F **Choose and write.**

-et	-en	-ed

G **Read the sentences three times.**

1 The **red** bag is **wet**. ☐ ☐ ☐

2 The **vet** has a **pen**. ☐ ☐ ☐

3 **Ten hen**s are on the **bed**. ☐ ☐ ☐

A Match and read.

1   f   •   •   og   •   •   🦊

2   l   •   •   ox   •   •   🧒

3   h   •   •   ot   •   •   🪵

B Circle the pictures with the same ending sounds.

1   fog

2   box

C Unscramble and write.

1

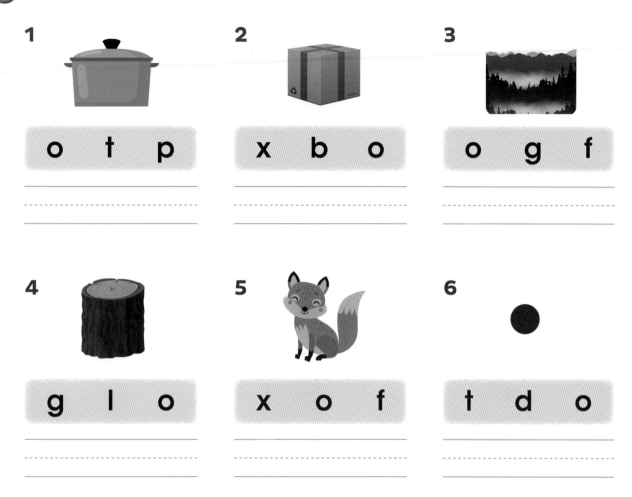

o   t   p

2

x   b   o

3

o   g   f

4

g   l   o

5

x   o   f

6

t   d   o

D Match the rhyming words.

1

2

E Trace and write.

1
hot

2
pot

3
dot

4
dog

5
log

6
fog

7
box

8
fox

9
ox

F Choose and write.

1	2	3	4
5	6	7	8

-ot

-ox

-og

G Read the sentences three times.

1   The **pot** is **hot**.   ☐ ☐ ☐

2   A **dog** is on the **log**.   ☐ ☐ ☐

3   The **box** has **dot**s.   ☐ ☐ ☐

A Match and read.

1 **c** · · **up** · ·

2 **b** · · **un** · ·

3 **r** · · **ug** · ·

B Circle the pictures with the same ending sounds.

1  **pup**

2  **sun**

C Unscramble and write.

1

n b u

_____

2

u p p

_____

3

u g r

_____

4

g h u

_____

5

p u c

_____

6

u n s

_____

D Match the rhyming words.

1

2

E Trace and write.

1

bug

2

hug

3

rug

4

up

5

cup

6

pup

7

sun

8

bun

9

run

F **Choose and write.**

-ug	-un	-up

G **Read the sentences three times.**

1   The **sun** is hot.   ☐ ☐ ☐

2   A **bug** is on the **cup**.   ☐ ☐ ☐

3   A **pup** **run**s to the **bun**.   ☐ ☐ ☐

Short Vowel u

A Match and read.

1   m ·   · ud ·   ·

2   c ·   · ub ·   ·

3   r ·   · ut ·   ·

B Circle and say.

1   ut

2   ud

3   ub

4   ut
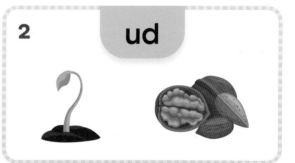

C Unscramble and write.

1

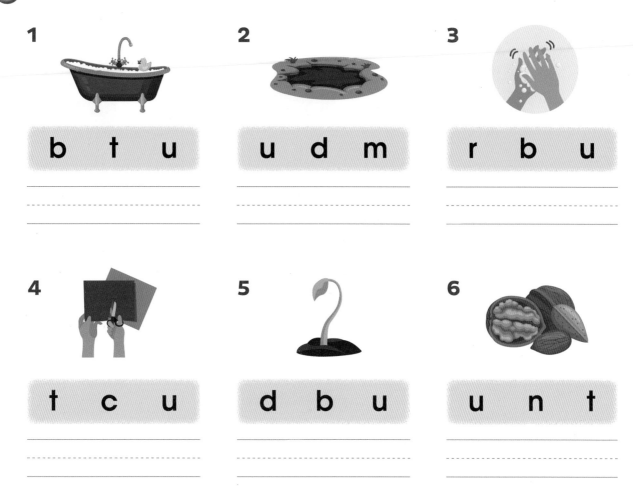

b	t	u

_____

2

u	d	m

_____

3

r	b	u

_____

4

t	c	u

_____

5

d	b	u

_____

6

u	n	t

_____

D Match the rhyming words.

1

2

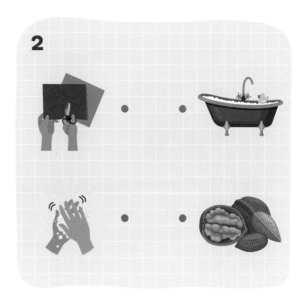

E **Trace and write.**

1
cut

2
nut

3
hut

4
bud

5
mud

6
tub

7
rub

Choose and write.

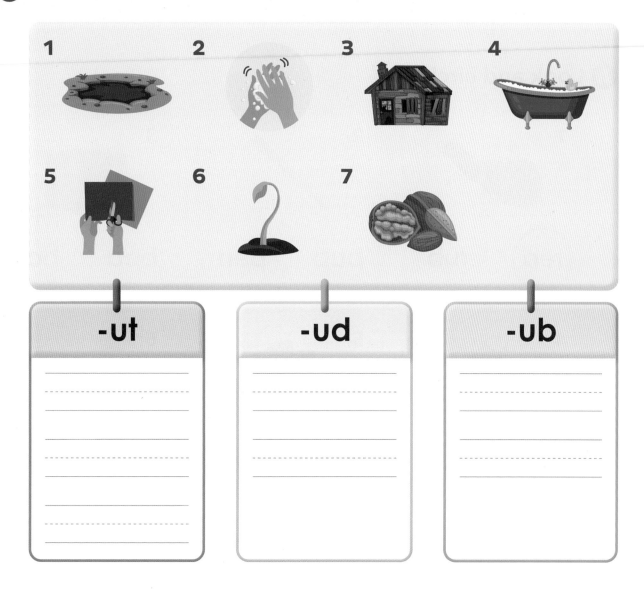

-ut

-ud

-ub

G **Read the sentences three times.**

1   A pig is in the **mud**.   ☐ ☐ ☐

2   A pup is in the **tub**.   ☐ ☐ ☐

3   The kids run to the **hut**.   ☐ ☐ ☐

A Look and circle.

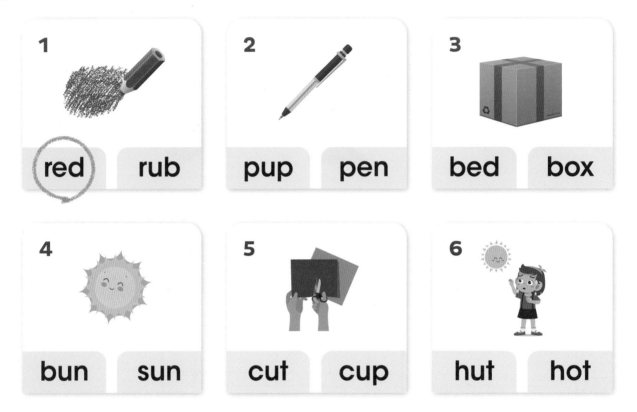

1. (red) rub
2. pup pen
3. bed box
4. bun sun
5. cut cup
6. hut hot

B Read and match.

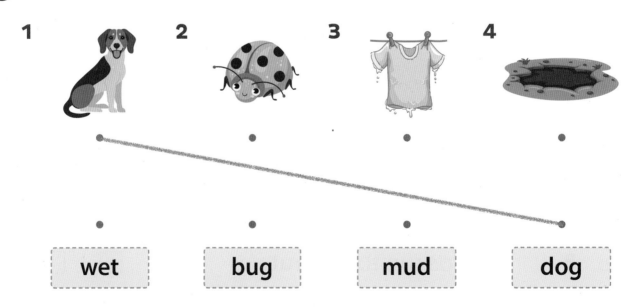

wet bug mud dog

C Choose, write, and say.

| et | en | og | ot | ub | un |

1

tub

2

d

3

b

4

l

5

t

6

h

7

r

8

r

9

w

10

h

11

v

12

f

D Find and circle.

1

b u w i g
t (h u g) q

2

e t c u p
d f h b c

3

c p e t y
p u b f i

4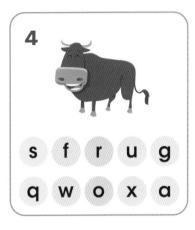

s f r u g
q w o x a

5

s h c b i
o h u t u

6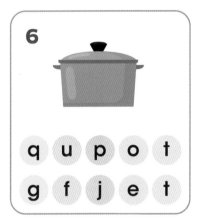

q u p o t
g f j e t

E Circle the pictures with the matching sound.

1

2

F **Read, circle, and write.**

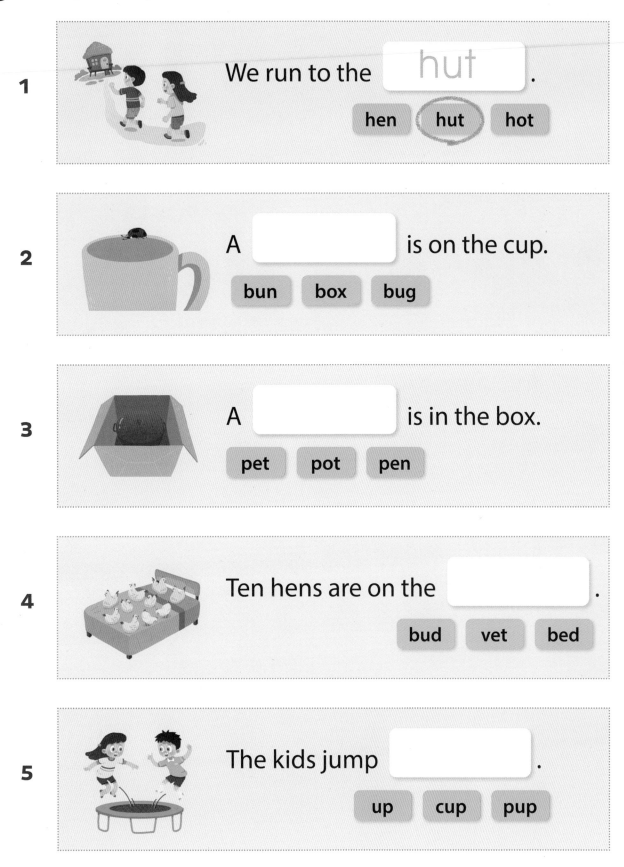

1. We run to the [hut] .

   hen (hut) hot

2. A _____ is on the cup.

   bun   box   bug

3. A _____ is in the box.

   pet   pot   pen

4. Ten hens are on the _____ .

   bud   vet   bed

5. The kids jump _____ .

   up   cup   pup

Oh! My Phonics is a four-level series of phonics books designed for EFL students to help them learn the fundamentals of phonics with efficient and practical methods. This series greatly assists young learners in understanding the relationship between letters and sounds effectively and adequately. *Oh! My Phonics* also introduces a number of common sight words embedded in fun phonics stories. In this way, children can naturally improve their sight word reading skills.

Oh! My Phonics Series

Alphabet Sounds

Short Vowels

Long Vowels

Double Letters

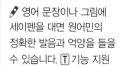

영어 문장이나 그림에 세이펜을 대면 원어민의 정확한 발음과 억양을 들을 수 있습니다. [T] 기능 지원

스토리에 등장한 각 Sight Word에 세이펜을 대면 원어민의 정확한 발음을 들을 수 있습니다.

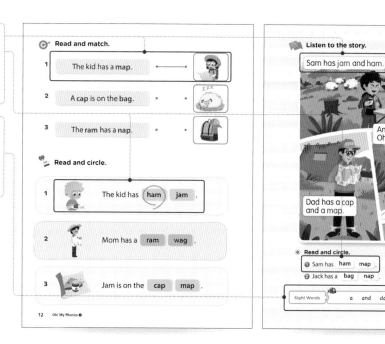

Listening 활동의 문제 번호에 펜을 대면 해당 문항의 음원이 재생됩니다.

각 단어나 그림에 세이펜을 대면 원어민의 정확한 발음과 억양을 들을 수 있습니다. [T] 기능 지원

각 글자에 세이펜을 대면 원어민의 정확한 발음을 들을 수 있습니다.

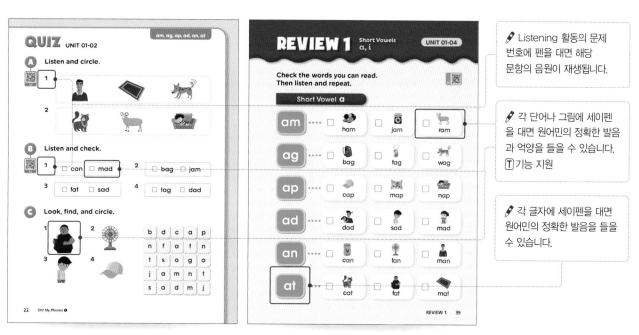

플래시카드의 각 단어나 그림에 세이펜을 대면 원어민의 정확한 발음과 억양을 들을 수 있습니다. [T] 기능 지원

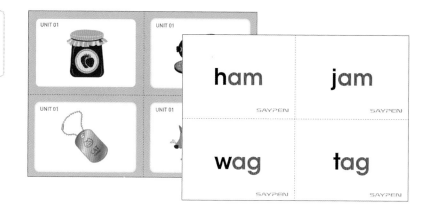

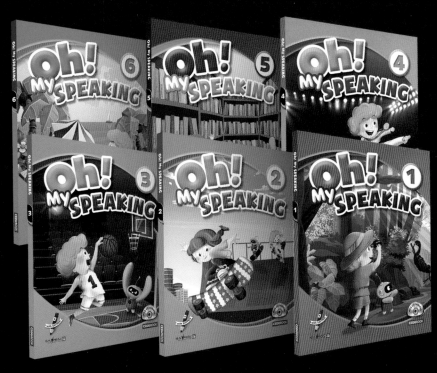